C000284698

Contents

INTRODUCTION

A good diet is an important part of your overall asthma treatment plan. Just like regular exercise, a healthy diet is good for everyone. That goes for people with asthma, too. Obesity is associated with more severe asthma, so you want to take steps to maintain a healthy weight.

There's evidence that people who eat diets higher in vitamins C and E, beta-carotene, flavonoids, magnesium, selenium, and omega-3 fatty acids have lower rates of asthma. Many of these substances are antioxidants, which protect cells from damage.

One recent study of asthma and diet showed that teens with poor nutrition were more likely to have asthma symptoms. Those who didn't get enough fruits and foods with vitamins C and E and omega-3 fatty acids were the most likely to have poor lung function. A 2007 study showed that children who grew up eating a Mediterranean diet high in nuts and fruits like grapes, apples, and tomatoes were less likely to have asthma.

RECIPES

Asthma Relief Recipes (Main Dishes)

Treat your taste buds to these delightful dishes and you'll also be doing your body a favor. The asthma relief recipes you find in this section of our Nutrition Guide for Asthma Sufferers are rich in nutrients that can help control and relieve asthma symptoms. Start cooking now!

Beet and Carrot Salad with Ginger

This recipe pairs two powerful root vegetables to create a powerful natural weapon for fighting asthma. Beets are packed with magnesium, which helps reduce constricted airways by relaxing the muscles around the bronchial tubes, while carrots are loaded with beta-carotene. In one study, women who ate the most carrots were found to have a 20% lower risk of asthma than women with the lowest intakes.

Serves 1

Ingredients
- 1/2 cup raw beets, peeled and grated
- 1/2 cup organic carrots, grated
- 2 tbsp apple juice

- 1 tbsp extra-virgin olive oil
- 1/2 tsp fresh ginger, minced
- 1/8 tsp sea salt

Directions
- Combine grated beets and carrots in a small bowl.
- Mix apple juice, olive oil, ginger, and salt in a separate bowl and drizzle over salad mixture. Toss gently. Enjoy!

Did you know?

Beta-carotene, found in many orange vegetables such as carrots, is a fat-soluble vitamin, which means that it has to be consumed together with a little bit of fat in order for it to be absorbed and utilized by the body. Therefore, the essential fatty acids provided by the olive oil in this recipe are an ideal accompaniment for carrots.

Zoodles with Mashed Avocado and Mediterranean Herbs

Starring mashed avocado and homemade zucchini noodles ("zoodles"), this simple gluten-free dish is jam-packed with glutathione and vitamin E, both of which are believed to fight asthma due to their strong antioxidant properties. This dish also contains garlic which may be good for asthma sufferers thanks to its ability to boost the body's production of prostacyclins, molecules that help keep the air passages of the lungs open. This Mediterranean-inspired recipe pairs zoodles with mashed avocado, garlic and Mediterranean herbs to create a creamy noodle-like dish that's full of flavor, antioxidants and essential fatty acids. Never heard of zoodles? Zoodles are basically just zucchini (courgette) cut into extra-thin, noodle-like strips. Naturally gluten-free, these imitation noodles make a great alternative to pasta for people who react adversely to grains and for those who follow a Paleo diet or another grain-free diet.

Note: This recipe uses yellow zucchini, which looks more like real noodles, but you can also use green zucchini to create this dish.

Serves 1

Ingredients
- 1 clove garlic
- Handful of fresh basil and oregano
- 1 avocado
- 1 yellow zucchini
- 1 Tbsp extra-virgin olive oil
- 1/4 cup water
- Salt, to taste

Directions

- Peel and chop the garlic, and set it aside while you prepare the rest of the ingredients. Preparing the garlic before the other ingredients helps improve its health benefits as allicin, the key active ingredient in garlic, takes some time to form after peeling and chopping.
- Rinse and chop the herbs and set them aside.
- Peel the avocado and remove the pit. Place the peeled and pitted avocado in a small bowl and mash thoroughly with a fork. Set aside.
- Wash the zucchini under cold running water, and cut it into long, thin noodle-shaped slices (zoodles) using a sturdy vegetable spiralizer, julienne slicer or electric zoodle maker. Set aside.
- Heat the olive oil in a skillet and saute the chopped garlic over medium heat for 1 minute. Add the zoodles and continue to saute for another minute or two, stirring frequently.
- Add the water and continue cooking for 4 more minutes, stirring occasionally.
- Remove the skillet from the heat, and let it cool slightly. Stir in the avocado, chopped herbs and salt, and serve immediately.

Beet and Carrot Soup

This recipe combines beets and carrots to create a beautiful crimson soup that is also rich in nutrients that can help relieve asthma symptoms. Beets are packed with magnesium, which helps heal constricted airways by relaxing the muscles around the bronchial tubes. Carrots, on the other hand, are one of the best dietary sources of the anti-asthma vitamin beta-carotene. In one study, women who consumed the most carrots were found to have a 20% lower risk of asthma than women with the lowest intakes.

Serves 4

Ingredients
- 3 medium beets, peeled and diced
- 1 tbsp olive oil
- 1 cup onion, chopped
- 1 pound carrots, diced
- 1 tbsp fresh ginger, minced
- 1 garlic clove, minced
- 6 cups vegetable stock

Directions
- Heat oil in a large saucepan over medium heat. Sauté onion until golden brown. Add ginger and garlic and cook for 2 minutes, stirring frequently.

- Add beets, carrots, and stock. Reduce heat to low and simmer covered until beets and carrots are tender, about 25 minutes.
- In a food processor, purée soup in batches. Taste soup and adjust seasonings.
- Serve hot or cold, garnished with cilantro leaves.

Omega-3 Omelet with Carrots and Tomatoes

Provided that your asthma is not linked to an allergy to eggs, this carotenoid-rich omelet can be of help in treating asthma. The carrots in this omelet are supercharged with beta-carotene while tomatoes are loaded with lycopene. Beta-carotene is a fat soluble antioxidant that combats free radicals which cause contraction of airway smooth muscles. Lycopene, another carotenoid with high antioxidant activity, has been shown to be particularly effective at controlling exercise-induced asthma.

Serves 4

Ingredients
- 2 tbsp extra virgin olive oil
- 1 bunch spring onions, sliced
- 4 tomatoes, diced
- 2/3 cup carrots, grated

- 8 eggs enriched with omega-3 fatty acids
- 2 tbsp nonfat natural yogurt
- 1/2 tsp dried marjoram

Directions

- Beat eggs and combine with rest of ingredients, except olive oil, in a large bowl.
- In a non-stick frying pan, heat olive oil. Pour in egg mixture. Cook until just set.
- Turn omelet over once. Transfer onto a plate and garnish as desired.

Omega-3 Omelet with Red Onions and Capers

Provided that you are not allergic or sensitive to eggs, this omelet may be of great help if you suffer from asthma. Onions, particularly red onions, as well as capers are among the best natural sources of quercetin, a bioflavonoid that has been shown to relieve asthma. What's more, this omelet provides plenty of omega-3 fatty acids which are known to have anti-inflammatory properties.

3 servings

Ingredients

- 4 large omega-3 enriched eggs
- 1 red onion, chopped
- 3 tsp capers
- 2 tbsp extra virgin olive oil
- 1 1/2 tbsp water
- 1/4 tsp salt

Directions

- Grease a non-stick frying pan with a paper towel dipped in extra-virgin olive oil. Add onion fry until almost golden.
- Beat eggs, water, and salt together in a small bowl. Add capers to mixture and pour over onions.
- Cook until egg is just set. Turn omelet over once.
- Transfer omelet onto a plate. Garnish as desired.

Green Pea and Mushroom Risotto

This simple recipe helps you create a risotto that's full of flavor and asthma-fighting minerals such as selenium. The beneficial effects of selenium on asthma are based on the role of this trace element in the antioxidant system of the body: selenium is a key component of several enzymes involved in antioxidant defense.

Serves 3

Ingredients

- 2 Tbsp olive oil
- 2/4 lb crimini mushrooms, cleaned, stemmed, diced
- 1 garlic clove, minced
- 1 yellow onion, finely chopped
- 1 2/3 cups long grain brown rice, uncooked
- 4 1/4 cups vegetable broth (allergen-free)
- 3 tbsp parsley, chopped
- 1/4 lb frozen peas, thawed
- Salt and pepper
- Fresh parsley, for garnish (optional)

Directions

- Heat 1 tablespoon olive oil in a large saucepan. Add mushrooms and season with salt and pepper. Cook, constantly stirring, for a few minutes until mushrooms soften. Transfer to a plate and set aside.
- Using same saucepan, heat another 1 tablespoon olive oil, and add minced garlic and onion. Sauté for a few minutes until onions begin to turn translucent. Add rice and cook for a few minutes, constantly stirring.
- Add half a cup of broth. Cook, stirring occasionally, until almost all broth is absorbed. Add another half a cup of broth each time

liquid is absorbed until all broth is used and rice is almost cooked (use water if you run out of broth towards end).

- Add peas, chopped parsley, and sautéed mushrooms. Cook for a few minutes, constantly stirring. Season with salt and pepper to taste. Transfer to serving plates and garnish with fresh parsley.

Ginger and Cucumber Salad

Ginger, one of the oldest spices in the world, is well known for its cold treating powers, but it may also help alleviate asthma symptoms. These asthma fighting properties of ginger are thought to be attributable to gingerols, strong anti-inflammatory substances that also give ginger its distinctive flavor.

Serves 4

Ingredients

- 2 cucumbers, diced
- 2 tbsp rice wine vinegar
- 1 tsp agave nectar
- 1 tbsp canola oil
- 1/3 cup pickled ginger, drained
- Chopped mint leaves, to taste
- Salt to taste

Directions

- In a medium bowl, combine diced cucumbers and ginger.
- Whisk together vinegar, agave nectar, canola oil, and mint leaves. Pour over cucumbers and ginger. Toss and season with salt. Let marinate refrigerated for 3 hours.
- Divide onto plates, and garnish as desired.

Salmon Salad

Salmon is rich in omega-3 fatty acids which have strong anti-inflammatory properties. Also tomatoes and onions contain many extraordinary properties that make them exceptional at preventing asthma and alleviating asthma symptoms.

Serves 4

Ingredients

- 2 large fillets (9 oz) wild salmon, either poached or grilled and chilled in the fridge until cool
- 1 cup cherry tomatoes, halved
- 2 red onions, sliced
- 1 tbsp capers
- 1 tablespoon fresh dill, finely chopped

- 1 tbsp balsamic vinegar
- 1 tbsp olive oil
- 1/4 tsp pepper, freshly ground
- Pinch of salt

Directions

- When salmon is cool, remove skin and bones. Break into chunks and add to a bowl.
- Add tomatoes, red onion, and capers. Toss.
- Mix vinegar, olive oil, and dill in a small bowl and add pour over salmon chunks. Toss again.
- Add salt and pepper to taste. Refrigerate for at least 30 minutes before serving.

Carrot and Avocado Salad

Avocados are well known for their contribution to beautiful skin, but these delicious creamy fruits can also be help alleviate asthma symptoms. Avocados are at the top of the list of foods with the highest concentration of glutathione, an unsung health promoting compound with widespread functions. Glutathione has been shown to protect cells against free radical damage and to detoxify foreign substances such as pollutants. Further, without glutathione other antioxidants could not function efficiently.

Avocados are also a good source of vitamin E, particularly for people whose asthma is linked to a nut allergy (nuts are one of the most common healthy sources of vitamin E).

2 servings

Ingredients

- 1 large avocado, peeled, pitted and diced
- 4 medium carrots, peeled and grated
- Dash of balsamic vinegar
- Sunflower seeds, to taste
- Salt and freshly ground pepper, to taste

Directions

- Combine avocado and grated carrots in a medium salad bowl. Sprinkle with sunflower seeds, salt, pepper, and balsamic vinegar.
- Cover and refrigerate for at least 20 minutes before serving.

Arugula, Avocado and Tomato Salad

The glutathione and vitamin E in avocados protects cells against free radical damage. Also the tomatoes in this salad may help alleviate asthma symptoms. In one study with 32 asthmatic adults, those who were given tomato extract rich in lycopene had a lower rate of lung inflammation than those who received a placebo.

4 servings

Ingredients

- 3 cups young arugula leaves, rinsed
- 2 cups cherry tomatoes, halved
- 1/4 cup sun-dried tomatoes, chopped
- 2 tablespoons extra virgin olive oil
- 1 tablespoon balsamic vinegar
- 2 small avocados, peeled, pitted and sliced

Directions

- In a large plastic bowl with a lid, combine arugula, cherry tomatoes, sun-dried tomatoes, olive oil, and vinegar. Toss well.
- Divide onto plates, and top each serving with slices of avocado.

Carrot Fennel Cucumber Salad

Provided that you're not allergic to lemon juice, this refreshing salad works like magic to soothe your soul—and bronchial airways. The airway soothing properties of this salad are due to the wide range of anti-asthma nutrients found in this salad. These nutrients include rosmarinic acid, omega-3 fatty acids, beta-carotene, potassium, vitamin C, and vitamin E.

4 servings

Ingredients

- 6 organic carrots, thinly sliced
- 1 fennel bulb, thinly sliced
- 1 cucumber, thinly sliced
- 1/2 cup fresh mint, chopped
- 4 Tbsp freshly squeezed lemon juice
- 2 Tbsp canola oil

Directions

- Combine carrots, fennel, cucumber, and mint in a large bowl.
- Mix lemon juice and canola oil in a container with a securable lid. Tighten lid and shake.
- Pour dressing over salad and toss gently

Breakfast Recipes for Fighting Asthma

Do you need of ideas for breakfast dishes that can help prevent and control asthma? If so, you have come to the right place. In this section of the Guide to Fighting Asthma you will find breakfast recipes that call for foods rich in nutrients that are thought to be effective at fighting asthma: According to a British study, children who eat just one banana a day had a 34% lower chance of developing asthmatic symptoms such as wheezing. The results where not surprising considering that bananas are one of the best sources of pyridoxine, commonly known as vitamin B6. Pyridoxine plays a critical role in the production of certain molecules that have been shown to help relax bronchial smooth muscle tissue.

Whole wheat Muffins with Bananas and Walnuts

Not only are these whole wheat breakfast muffins full of flavor, they also contain ingredients that help fight asthma. Bananas help relax bronchial smooth muscle tissue, and walnuts can help fight asthma attacks due to their anti-inflammatory properties.

Makes 6-8 muffins

Ingredients

- 1 cup whole wheat flour
- 1/3 cup brown sugar
- 1/2 tsp baking powder
- 2/3 cup walnuts, chopped
- 1/4 tsp salt
- 2 medium bananas, sliced
- 1/4 cup almond milk
- 1 egg, lightly beaten

Directions

- Preheat oven to 350°F (175°C, gas 4).
- Combine flour, sugar, baking powder, walnuts, and salt. In a separate bowl, mash bananas with a fork.
- Add egg and almond milk to banana mixture, then combine dry and wet ingredients. Pour batter into a non-stick muffin pan.
- Bake for 30-40 minutes, then transfer muffins to a cooling rack. Serve warm.

Antioxidant Muffins

These scrumptious muffins feature blueberries and pecans, two antioxidant powerhouse foods. Blueberries top the list of berries with the highest antioxidant capacity, and pecans—along with walnuts and chestnuts—have the highest concentration of antioxidants in the tree nut family.

Makes 6-8 muffins

Ingredients
- 1 cup whole wheat flour
- 1/3 cup brown sugar
- 1/2 tsp baking powder
- 1/3 cup pecans, chopped
- 1/4 tsp salt
- 1 cup blueberries
- 1/4 cup almond milk
- 1 large egg

Directions
- Preheat oven to 350°F (175°C, gas 4).
- Combine flour, sugar, baking powder, pecans, and salt. In a separate bowl, lightly beat egg and almond milk. Combine dry and wet ingredients.
- Pour batter into paper muffin cups. Bake for 30-40 minutes, then transfer muffins to a cooling rack. Serve warm.

Carrot Muffins

You've probably heard that carrots are good for vision, but did you know that they may also be helpful for people susceptible to asthma? In one study, women who ate the most carrots were found to have a 20% lower risk of asthma than women with the lowest intakes. These beneficial effects are likely to be linked to high concentration of beta-carotene in carrots, but also the vitamin C contained in carrots may play a role.

Yields 12 muffins

Ingredients

- 1 egg
- 1 cup rice milk
- 4 tbsp canola oil
- 2 cups quinoa flour or other gluten-free flour
- 1 tsp guar gum
- 1 tbsp flaxseed meal
- 3 1/2 tsp gluten-free baking powder
- 1/2 tsp salt
- 1 tsp cinnamon
- 1/4 cup brown sugar
- 1 cup organic carrots, grated

- 1/4 cup raisins

Directions

- Preheat oven to 400 degrees F (200 degrees C, gas mark 6)
- Beat together egg, rice milk, and canola oil. Combine dry ingredients in a separate bowl.
- Add liquid ingredients to dry ingredients and mix until just blended (do not over-mix). Fold in grated carrots and raisins.
- Fill 12 paper muffin cups with batter (about two thirds full). Bake for 20 minutes.

Buckwheat Pancakes with Bananas

Unlike most other pancake recipes, this one requires neither eggs nor dairy, making this dessert generally suitable for people with asthma (eggs and dairy are among the most common food triggers of asthma attacks). All key ingredients in this dessert—buckwheat, bananas, and brown rice syrup—are considered hypoallergenic, which means that they are among the foods that are least likely to cause allergic reactions in humans. In addition, bananas have been shown to have strong asthma-fighting qualities.

Serves 2

Ingredients

- 1 cup buckwheat flour
- 1 Tbsp brown sugar
- 2 Tbsp potato starch
- 1/2 tsp salt
- 1 tsp baking powder
- 1 cup rice milk
- 2 Tbsp canola oil
- Vegetable cooking spray, for frying
- 2 large bananas, sliced
- Brown rice syrup, to serve

Directions

- Combine dry ingredients in a medium bowl. Add rice milk and canola oil, and whisk until well combined. If batter seems very thick, you may want add a little extra rice milk or water.
- Preheat a large nonstick skillet over medium heat. Spray with vegetable cooking spray.
- With a ladle, pour batter to the size you prefer. Even out batter on skillet with back of a spoon. Cook pancake on medium high heat for a few minutes until bubbles appear. Flip over and continue

frying until cooked (a properly cooked pancake appears dense and not sticky when cut in the middle).

- Repeat previous step until batter is gone.
- Serve pancakes with banana slices and brown rice syrup.

Original Bircher Muesli

Muesli was developed as a health food by the Swiss Physician Maximilian Bircher-Brenner towards the end of the 19th century. This is the original muesli recipe Mr Bircher-Benner recommended to his patients.

1 serving

Ingredients
- 1 tbsp rolled oats
- 3 tbsp water
- 1 tbsp sweetened condensed milk
- 2 tsp lemon juice
- 1-2 apples (including skin)
- 1 tbsp hazelnuts or almonds, ground

Directions
- Combine oats and water and refrigerate overnight. Soaking improves the nutritional value of oats as it allows enzymes to

break down and neutralize phytic acid, a compound that can block the absorption of many minerals in the intestines.

- Grate apples. Add them, together with sweetened condensed milk and lemon juice, to soaked oats. Stir well.
- Sprinkle with almonds or hazelnuts and serve.

Did you know?

Soaking improves the nutritional value of oats as it allows enzymes to break down and neutralize phytic acid, a compound that can block the absorption of many minerals in the intestines.

Oat and Buckwheat Muesli with Pears and Grapes

Indulging in a bowl of this super-healthy muesli for breakfast is an excellent way to start a day. Pears, a key ingredient in this breakfast dish, have been shown to protect against asthma. Also resveratrol, a substance found in the skins of red grapes, may help asthma sufferers.

4 servings

Ingredients

- 1 1/2 cups rolled oats
- 1/2 cup puffed buckwheat

- 1/2 cup dried apples, chopped
- 2 tsp ground cinnamon 1 cup organic pears, diced
- 1 cup red grapes, halved
- 3 tbsp brown sugar
- Rice milk to serve

Directions

- Preheat oven to 325°F (160°C, gas 3).
- Spread oats evenly onto a non-stick baking tray and toast in preheated oven for about 10 minutes, stirring occasionally. Watch oats very closely when toasting as they can burn easily.
- Remove from oven and let cool. Pour into a large ceramic or glass bowl and add water. Let soak in a refrigerator overnight.
- Add puffed buckwheat, dried apples, cinnamon, and brown sugar to soaked oats. Stir well.
- Divide mixture into serving bowls and top with pears and grapes. Serve with rice milk.

Oat Muesli with Apples and Raspberries

This dairy-free recipe features apples and raspberries, two great sources of quercetin. Quercetin is a bioflavonoid that is known to possess strong antioxidant, anti-histamine, and anti-inflammatory properties which help alleviate asthma.

4 servings

Ingredients

- 1 1/2 cups rolled oats
- 1/2 cup popped rice
- 2 tsp ground cinnamon
- 1 cup organic apples, diced
- 1 cup raspberries
- 3 tbsp brown sugar
- Rice milk to serve

Directions

- Preheat oven to 325°F (160°C, gas 3).
- Mix oats, sugar, and cinnamon in a bowl. Spread mixture evenly onto a non-stick baking tray.
- Toast oat mixture in preheated oven for about 10 minutes, stirring occasionally. Watch mixture very closely when toasting as it can burn very easily.
- Remove from oven and let cool. Pour into a large bowl and stir in popped rice.
- Divide mixture into serving bowls and top with apples and raspberries. Serve with rice milk.

Omega-3 Omelet with Red Onions and Capers

Provided that you are not allergic or sensitive to eggs, this omelet may be of great help if you suffer from asthma. Onions, particularly red onions, as well as capers are among the best natural sources of quercetin, a bioflavonoid that has been shown to relieve asthma. What's more, this omelet provides plenty of omega-3 fatty acids which are known to have anti-inflammatory properties

3 servings

Ingredients

- 4 large omega-3 enriched eggs
- 1 red onion, chopped
- 3 tsp capers
- 2 tbsp extra virgin olive oil
- 1 1/2 tbsp water
- 1/4 tsp salt

Directions

- Grease a non-stick frying pan with a paper towel dipped in extra-virgin olive oil. Add onion fry until almost golden.

- Beat eggs, water, and salt together in a small bowl. Add capers to mixture and pour over onions.
- Cook until egg is just set. Turn omelet over once.
- Transfer omelet onto a plate. Garnish as desired.

Omega-3 Omelet with Carrots and Tomatoes

Provided that your asthma is not linked to an allergy to eggs, this carotenoid-rich breakfast omelet can be of help in treating asthma. The carrots in this omelet are brimming with beta-carotene while tomatoes are packed with lycopene. Beta-carotene is a fat soluble antioxidant that combats free radicals which cause contraction of airway smooth muscles. Lycopene, another carotenoid with high antioxidant activity, has been shown to be particularly effective at controlling exercise-induced asthma.

Serves 4

Ingredients

- 2 tbsp extra virgin olive oil
- 1 bunch spring onions, sliced
- 4 tomatoes, diced

- 2/3 cup carrots, grated
- 8 eggs enriched with omega-3 fatty acids
- 2 tbsp nonfat natural yogurt
- 1/2 tsp dried marjoram

Directions

- Beat eggs and combine with rest of ingredients, except olive oil, in a large bowl.
- In a non-stick frying pan, heat olive oil. Pour in egg mixture. Cook until just set.
- Turn omelet over once. Transfer onto a plate and garnish as desired.

Dessert Recipes for Fighting Asthma

Treat your taste buds to these delightful desserts designed to ease symptoms in asthma sufferers. The dessert recipes you find in this section of our Nutrition Guide for Asthma Sufferers are rich in nutrients that can help control asthma symptoms.

Asthma-Fighting Banana and Apple Smoothie

In one study, children who consumed apple juice daily were half as likely to suffer from wheezing as those who drank it less than once a month. Bananas were found to exert a similar, albeit a weaker, benefit.

2 servings

One study found that children who consumed apple juice daily were half as likely to suffer from wheezing as those who drank it less than once a month. Bananas were found to exert a similar, albeit a weaker, benefit.

Ingredients

- 1 frozen banana, peeled and chopped
- 1 cup apple juice

Directions

- Combine banana and apple juice in a blender or food processor. Process until smooth.
- Pour into glasses and serve with non-plastic straws which are good both for you and the environment

Raspberry Banana Smoothie

This dairy-free smoothie is bursting with vitamin B6, potassium, vitamin C, and quercetin. What's more, both the raspberries and the ground flaxseed add healthful omega-3 fatty acids to this delectable anti-asthma smoothie.

2 servings

Ingredients

- 1 cup fresh raspberries
- 1 ripe banana, sliced and frozen
- 1 cup rice milk
- 1 Tbsp flaxseed, freshly ground

Directions

- Combine all ingredients in a blender or food processor and process until smooth.

- Garnish as desired, and serve with eco-friendly straws made of stainless steel, glass, or bamboo.

Watermelon and Green Tea Smoothie

This refreshing smoothie is perfect for the summer heat. But it is also great for people with asthma as watermelon is literally brimming with lycopene, a type of carotenoid that has been shown to be particularly effective at controlling exercise-induced asthma. In addition to lycopene, this drink contains plenty of beta-carotene, vitamin C, potassium, and magnesium.

4 servings

Ingredients

- 3 cups watermelon, seeded, chopped
- 1 cup nonfat yoghurt containing probiotic bacteria, cold
- 1/2 cup green tea brewed from loose leaves, chilled
- 1 tbsp fresh mint, minced
- Lemon juice, freshly pressed

Directions

- Combine all ingredients in a blender or food processor and process until creamy.
- Garnish as desired. Serve in tall glasses with quirky eco-straws made of bamboo, stainless steel, or glass.

Buckwheat Pancakes with Bananas

Unlike most other pancake recipes, this one requires neither eggs nor dairy, making this dessert generally suitable for people with asthma (eggs and dairy are among the most common food triggers of asthma attacks). All key ingredients in this devine dessert—buckwheat, bananas, and brown rice syrup—are considered hypoallergenic, which means that they are among the foods that are least likely to cause allergic reactions in humans. In addition, bananas have been shown to have strong asthma-fighting qualities.

Serves 2

Ingredients

- 1 cup buckwheat flour
- 1 Tbsp brown sugar
- 2 Tbsp potato starch
- 1/2 tsp salt

- 1 tsp baking powder
- 1 cup rice milk
- 2 Tbsp canola oil
- Vegetable cooking spray, for frying
- 2 large bananas, sliced
- Brown rice syrup, to serve

Directions

- Combine dry ingredients in a medium bowl. Add rice milk and canola oil, and whisk until well combined. If batter seems very thick, you may want add a little extra rice milk or water.
- Preheat a large nonstick skillet over medium heat. Spray with vegetable cooking spray.
- With a ladle, pour batter to the size you prefer. Even out batter on skillet with back of a spoon. Cook pancake on medium high heat for a few minutes until bubbles appear. Flip over and continue frying until cooked (a properly cooked pancake appears dense and not sticky when cut in the middle).
- Repeat previous step until batter is gone.
- Serve pancakes with banana slices and brown rice syrup.

Rice pudding with Pears and Cinnamon

Both rice and pears are among the least likely foods to cause allergic reactions, such as asthma attacks. In addition, a high consumption of pears has been linked to an increased protection against asthma.

8 servings

Ingredients

- 1 cup brown basmati rice 2 cups water

  1/2 teaspoon salt

  3 cups rice milk

  1/3 cup brown sugar

  1 tsp cinnamon, ground

  1 tbsp potato starch

  1 tsp vanilla extract

  4 organic pears, peeled, cored, and sliced

  Ground cinnamon, for garnish

- Place rice, water, and salt in a medium saucepan and bring to a boil. Reduce heat to low, cover, and simmer, stirring occasionally, until water is fully absorbed, about 45 minutes.

- Add rice milk, brown sugar, and cinnamon, and stir well. Continue cooking, stirring occasionally, for 10 minutes.

- Mix potato starch with a few drops of water in a small bowl and stir into rice mixture. Continue stirring over low heat until mixture thickens and reaches consistency of pudding, about 5 minutes. Remove from heat.
- Transfer to a large bowl, cover, and refrigerate until cold, about 2 hours. Divide into serving bowls and top with sliced pears. Garnish with cinnamon.

Did you know?

Conventionally grown pears typically contain high levels of pesticides and other harmful chemicals. Therefore, it is highly advisable to opt for organic produce when buying pears.

Low-Fat Apple and Raspberry Crumble

This gluten-free recipe combines apples and raspberries, two great sources of quercetin. Quercetin is a bioflavonoid that is known to possess strong antioxidant, anti-histamine, and anti-inflammatory properties which help alleviate asthma.

Dairy-Free

Ingredients

- 5 large cooking apples, finely sliced
- 1 cup raspberries

- 2 cups apple juice
- 2 cups rolled oats
- 2 tbsp butter or margarine
- 2 tbsp brown sugar
- 2 tsp of cinnamon
- 1/2 tsp cloves

Directions

- Preheat oven to 350°F (gas 4)
- Arrange apple slices and raspberries in a buttered baking dish. Pour apple juice over.
- Mix rolled oats, sugar, and spices in a medium bowl. Cut in butter or margarine with fingers until evenly dispersed.
- Cover apples and raspberries with crumble topping.
- Bake for 45-60 minutes in preheated oven. Serve hot or cold.

Apple Slices with Cinnamon

This dessert is a cinch to prepare, and it contains only 95 calories! It is also a great dessert for people with asthma due to the high concentration of quercetin found in apples. Quercetin is known to possess strong antioxidant, anti-histamine, and anti-inflammatory properties.

Serves 1

Ingredients

- 1 medium apple, cored and sliced
- 1/4 tsp cinnamon, ground

Directions

Place apple slices on a small serving plate. Sprinkle with cinnamon and serve immediately.

Chocolate Free "Chocolate" Pudding

Even if your asthma is linked to an allergy or intolerance to chocolate, you can still enjoy the irresistible sweetness and texture of a "chocolate" pudding — as long as it's made with carob, like this one! Carob flour, made from the pots of the carob tree, has a mild cocoa-like flavor but is considered hypoallergenic. In addition to carob, this pudding is rich in millet which is an excellent source of magnesium. A high intake of magnesium has been associated with a lower risk of asthma.

Ingredients

- 3/4 cup water
- 1/3 cup dates, chopped

- 1/8 tsp. salt
- 1/2 tsp vanilla
- 2 tbsp carob powder
- 1 1/3 cups hot cooked millet

Directions

- Mix water and dates in a food processor, and process until smooth. Transfer to a saucepan and bring to a boil.
- Remove from heat, and add rest of ingredients.
- Blend until smooth. Chill and serve.

Quinoa Crepes with Applesauce

Quinoa is considered one of the least allergenic of all grains, making it a great grain for people with asthma. The applesauce these crepes are served with can also be helpful: one study discovered that pregnant women who ate apples protected their child from developing asthma. Another study found that by drinking apple juice daily children could reduce their chance of suffering from wheezing by 50 percent.

10-12 crepes

Ingredients

- 1 1/2 quinoa flour

- 1/2 cup tapioca flour
- 1 tsp baking soda
- 1 tsp cinnamon
- 2 cup carbonated water
- 3 tbsp canola oil
- 3 cups unswtnd, organic apple sauce
- Cinnamon, to taste

Directions

- In a medium bowl, mix together quinoa flour, tapioca flour, baking soda, and cinnamon. Add water and oil and whisk until well combined.
- Preheat a large nonstick skillet over medium heat. Add a few drops of canola oil.
- For first crepe, pour about 1/3 cup of batter into skillet, rotating skillet quickly until bottom is evenly coated. Cook crepe on medium high heat until bottom is light brown. Flip over and briefly cook other side.
- Repeat previous step until batter is gone. Serve with apple sauce.

Pear Frost with Ginger

A vast body of evidence suggests that pears can provide increased protection against asthma. Also ginger is thought to aid in the treatment of asthma as it contains gingerols, strong anti-inflammatory substances that also give ginger its distinctive flavor.

2 servings

Ingredients

- 2 cup organic pears, peeled and chopped
- 1 cup apple juice
- 1 tsp fresh ginger root, grated
- 1 cup crushed ice

Directions

- Combine first three ingredients in a blender or food processor and process until smooth.
- Pour over crushed ice in tall glasses and garnish as desired. Serve with quirky eco-straws made of stainless steel, glass, or bamboo.

Salad Recipes for Asthmatics

Are you looking for ideas for salads that can help prevent and control symptoms in asthmatic adults and children? If so, you have come to the right place. In this section of HealWithFood.org'sNutrition Guide to Fighting Asthma you will find salad recipes that call for anti-asthma foods, that is, foods that are considered suitable for asthma sufferers.

Super-Nutritious Broccoli Salad with Apples and Cranberries

This super healthy salad combines ingredients that provide substantial amounts of anti-asthma nutrients such as beta-carotene, vitamin C, vitamin E, selenium, magnesium, potassium, and quercetin. What's more, it contains some omega-3 fatty acids (provided by the broccoli). Note: this recipe contains dairy.

6 servings

This low-GI broccoli salad featuring apples and cranberries is low in calories and low in fat, but loaded with a wide range of nutrients.

Ingredients

- 4 cups fresh broccoli florets
- 1/2 cup dried cranberries

- 1/2 cup sunflower seeds
- 3 organic apples
- 1/4 cup red onion, chopped
- 1 cup plain, low-fat yoghurt with probiotic bacteria
- 2 Tbsp Dijon style mustard
- 1/4 cup honey

Directions

- Combine broccoli florets, dried cranberries, sunflower seeds, chopped apples, and chopped onion in a large serving bowl. Blend yoghurt, mustard, and honey in a small bowl.
- Add dressing to the salad and toss. Chill before serving.

Romaine and Smoked Salmon Salad

Romaine lettuce and carrots provide an abundance of beta-carotene and vitamin C, both of which help alleviate asthma symptoms due to their antioxidant powers. Salmon and radishes are also beneficial as they possess strong anti-inflammatory properties.

Serves 2

Ingredients

- 1 small head organic romaine lettuce

- 5 ounces smoked salmon, thinly sliced
- 2 tomatoes, diced
- 4 radishes, thinly sliced
- 1 organic carrot, diagonally sliced
- 1/2 cucumber, peeled and diced
- Juice of half a lemon
- 1 tsp fresh ginger root, peeled and minced
- 1 tbsp canola oil

Directions

- Arrange romaine lettuce on two plates. Top with salmon, tomatoes, radishes, carrots, and cucumber.
- Shake lemon juice, canola oil, and minced ginger in tightly covered jar. Pour over salad.

Tomato, Cucumber and Red Onion Salad

Tomatoes are known to possess several extraordinary properties that make them exceptional at preventing asthma and alleviating asthma symptoms. Their most notable quality: they contain lycopene which can reduce lung inflammation in asthmatic adults. Red onions, another key ingredient in this salad, possess strong anti-inflammatory properties which may also help alleviate asthma in some people.

Ingredients

- 2 large cucumbers, peeled and coarsely chopped
- 3 large tomatoes, coarsely chopped
- 2/3 cup red onion, coarsely chopped
- 1/3 cup balsamic vinegar
- 1/2 tbsp white sugar
- 3 tablespoons extra virgin olive oil
- Salt and pepper, to taste
- Fresh basil or mint leaves, for garnish (optional)

Directions

- In a large bowl with a lid, combine all ingredients. Cover, and shake to mix.
- Season with salt and pepper.

Salmon Salad

Salmon is rich in omega-3 fatty acids which have strong anti-inflammatory properties. Also tomatoes and onions contain several extraordinary properties that make them exceptional at preventing asthma and alleviating asthma symptoms.

Serves 4

Ingredients

- 2 large fillets (9 oz) wild salmon, either poached or grilled and chilled in the fridge until cool
- 1 cup cherry tomatoes, halved
- 2 red onions, sliced
- 1 tbsp capers
- 1 tablespoon fresh dill, finely chopped
- 1 tbsp balsamic vinegar
- 1 tbsp olive oil
- 1/4 tsp pepper, freshly ground
- Pinch of salt

Directions

- When salmon is cool, remove skin and bones. Break into chunks and add to a bowl.
- Add tomatoes, red onion, and capers. Toss.
- Mix vinegar, olive oil, and dill in a small bowl and add pour over salmon chunks. Toss again.
- Add salt and pepper to taste. Refrigerate for at least 30 minutes before serving.

Carrot and Avocado Salad

Avocados are well known for their contribution to beautiful skin, but these delicious creamy fruits can also be help alleviate asthma symptoms. Avocados are at the top of the list of foods with the highest concentration of glutathione, an unsung health promoting compound with widespread functions. Glutathione has been shown to protect cells against free radical damage and to detoxify foreign substances such as pollutants. Further, without glutathione other antioxidants could not function efficiently. Avocados are also a good source of vitamin E, particularly for people whose asthma is linked to a nut allergy (nuts are one of the most common healthy sources of vitamin E).

2 servings

Ingredients

- 1 large avocado, peeled, pitted and diced
- 4 medium carrots, peeled and grated
- Dash of balsamic vinegar
- Sunflower seeds, to taste
- Salt and freshly ground pepper, to taste

Directions

- Combine avocado and grated carrots in a medium salad bowl. Sprinkle with sunflower seeds, salt, pepper, and balsamic vinegar.
- Cover and refrigerate for at least 20 minutes before serving.

Carrot Fennel Cucumber Salad

Provided that you're not allergic to citrus fruits, this summery salad works like magic to soothe your soul—and bronchial airways. The airway soothing properties of this salad are due to the wide range of anti-asthma nutrients found in this salad. These nutrients include rosmarinic acid, omega-3 fatty acids, beta-carotene, potassium, and vitamin C, and vitamin E.

4 servings

Ingredients

- 6 organic carrots, thinly sliced
- 1 fennel bulb, thinly sliced
- 1 cucumber, thinly sliced
- 1/2 cup fresh mint, chopped
- 4 Tbsp freshly squeezed lemon juice
- 2 Tbsp canola oil

Directions

- Combine carrots, fennel, cucumber, and mint in a large bowl.
- Mix lemon juice and canola oil in a container with a securable lid. Tighten lid and shake.
- Pour dressing over salad and toss gently.

Beet and Carrot Salad with Ginger

This recipe pairs two powerful root vegetables to create an excellent natural remedy for fighting asthma. Beets are packed with magnesium, which helps reduce constricted airways by relaxing the muscles around the bronchial tubes, while carrots are loaded with beta-carotene. In one study, women who ate the most carrots were found to have a 20% lower risk of asthma than women with the lowest intakes.

Serves 1

Ingredients
- 1/2 cup raw beets, peeled and grated
- 1/2 cup organic carrots, grated
- 2 tbsp apple juice
- 1 tbsp extra-virgin olive oil
- 1/2 tsp fresh ginger, minced
- 1/8 tsp sea salt

Directions

- Combine grated beets and carrots in a small bowl.
- Mix apple juice, olive oil, ginger, and salt in a separate bowl and drizzle over salad mixture. Toss gently. Enjoy!

Did you know?

Beta-carotene, found in many orange vegetables such as carrots, is a fat-soluble vitamin, which means that it has to be consumed together with a little bit of fat in order for it to be absorbed and utilized by the body. Therefore, the essential fatty acids provided by the olive oil in this recipe are an ideal accompaniment for carrots.

Chicken and Apple Salad

This recipe pair's juicy chicken with crunchy apples and luscious grapes to create a culinary hit that is sure to please almost everyone. Chicken, apples, and grapes rarely cause allergic reactions, so this salad is also well suited for those who suffer from asthma. In addition, the apples in this salad possess some extraordinary properties that may be protective against asthma. One study discovered that pregnant women who ate apples protected their child from developing asthma. Another study found that by drinking apple juice daily children could reduce their chance of suffering from wheezing by 50 percent.

Serves 4

Ingredients

- 3 cups cooked chicken, diced
- 1 cup grapes, halved
- 1/2 cup celery, diced
- 3 tbsp red onion, finely chopped
- 1/2 cup organic apples, diced
- 6 tbsp extra light mayonnaise
- 2 tsp lemon juice
- Salt and pepper, to taste
- Lettuce leaves

Directions

- Combine first five ingredients in a large bowl.
- In a small bowl, combine mayonnaise, lemon juice, and salt and pepper. Stir into chicken mix.
- Arrange lettuce leaves on serving plates and top with chicken salad.

Anti-Asthma Soup Recipes for Asthma Prevention

Are you looking for soup recipes featuring foods that are suitable for asthma sufferers? This section of HealWithFood.org'sNutrition Guide to Fighting Asthma provides anti-asthma soup recipes that call for foods with asthma fighting properties.

Carrot, Tomato and Lentil Soup

This carotenoid-rich soup is suitable for asthmatics and can even help alleviate asthma symptoms. The carrots in this soup deliver a good wallop of beta-carotene while tomatoes provide a generous amount of lycopene. Beta-carotene is a fat soluble antioxidant that combats free radicals which cause contraction of airway smooth muscles. Lycopene, another carotenoid with high antioxidant activity, has been shown to be particularly effective at controlling exercise-induced asthma.

Serves 4

Ingredients

- 2 tbsp extra virgin olive oil
- 1 large yellow onion, sliced
- 2 carrots, diced

- 2 cloves garlic
- 1 tsp ground ginger
- 2 tsp ground cumin
- 2 tsp ground coriander seeds
- 1 cup red lentils
- 28 oz (420g) canned tomatoes
- 6 cups vegetable stock
- 1 1/2 tsp salt
- 1/2 tsp black pepper, freshly ground
- Greek style yoghurt, to serve (optional)

Directions

- Peel and crush garlic and set aside. Leaving crushed or minced garlic for at least 5-10 minutes after crushing helps maximize its health-protective effects.
- While health-promoting compounds are forming in crushed garlic, heat olive oil in a large nonstick saucepan over medium heat. Add onion and cook for 3 minutes, stirring occasionally.
- Add stock, lentils, canned tomatoes, carrots, ginger, cumin, coriander, salt, and pepper, and bring to boil. Cover pot and let simmer for 25 minutes over medium heat.
- Add garlic and let simmer for another 5 minutes.

- Working in batches, purée soup in a blender or use an immersible hand blender to process soup until smooth.
- Spoon soup into bowls and top with a generous dollop of yoghurt.

Dairy-Free Spinach Soup

This delicious, vibrant green spinach soup draws on the health benefits of spinach. Research shows that people with a high intake of spinach generally have a lower risk of developing asthma. This is not surprising considering that spinach features a host of important asthma preventing nutrients, including beta-carotene, vitamin C, vitamin E, and magnesium. It also has substantial potassium content in proportion to its calorie content: a 100 calorie serving provides about 40% of the reference daily intake for this important asthma-fighting mineral.

4 servings

Ingredients

- 10 oz fresh spinach
- 2 tbsp olive oil
- 1 yellow onion, chopped
- 4 cups vegetable stock
- 3 tbsp corn starch

- Dash of ground nutmeg
- Salt to taste
- Optional: chopped fresh chives, for garnish

Directions

- Wash spinach thoroughly. Drain and chop coarsely.
- Heat olive oil and sauté onion in a large saucepan until golden brown.
- Add stock and spinach, and bring to a boil. Cook until spinach is tender. Blend with a hand held blender until smooth.
- Put two tablespoons of flour into a small bowl and add just enough warm to dissolve the flour. Use a small whisk to mix flour with water until you have a runny paste. Add half a cup of warm water to the bowl and mix. Pour mixture into saucepan and whisk to blend thoroughly.
- Let simmer on low to medium heat for a few minutes, until thickened. Season with nutmeg and salt. Remove from heat.
- Pour soup into serving bowls and garnish with chopped chives, if desired. Serve immediately.

Simple Sweet Potato Ginger Soup

Sweet potatoes are one of the vegetables that are least likely to cause allergic reactions such as asthma attacks. What's more, sweet potatoes contain many compounds that may even help fight attacks triggered by other substances. Also the onions this recipe calls for may be helpful for people with asthma because of the high amount of quercetin onions contain. Furthermore, ginger may be helpful because it contains gingerols, strong anti-inflammatory substances that also give ginger its distinctive flavor.

6-8 servings

Ingredients

- 1 Tbsp olive oil
- 2 medium yellow onions, chopped
- 3 large sweet potatoes (pink, orange, or yellow variety), peeled and chopped
- 1 inch piece fresh ginger, peeled and finely chopped
- 6 cups low-sodium vegetable broth
- Salt and pepper, to taste

Directions

- Heat oil in a medium saucepan over medium heat. Add onions and sauté until golden.

- Pour in the broth and bring to boil over medium-high heat. Add sweet potatoes and ginger, and reduce heat to medium-low. Simmer until sweet potatoes are easily pierced with a fork (about 20 to 25 minutes).
- Working in batches, purée soup in a blender or use an immersible hand blender to blend soup until smooth. Season with salt and pepper to taste. Serve hot.

Tangy Tomato Soup with Basil

Tomatoes possess many properties that make them exceptional at preventing asthma and alleviating asthma symptoms. Their most interesting quality: they contain lycopene. In one study with 32 asthmatic adults, those who were given tomato extract rich in lycopene had a lower rate of lung inflammation than those who received a placebo. Lycopene from processed tomato products — such as the stewed tomatoes used in this soup — appears to be more bioavailable than lycopene from raw tomatoes. Also the basil this recipe calls for contributes to the asthma fighting power of this soup as it is rich in flavonoids which provide antioxidant protection.

2 servings

Ingredients

- 3 large garlic cloves
- 3 oz shallots, peeled sliced
- 1 Tbsp olive oil
- 1 (14 1/2-ounce) can stewed tomatoes, undrained
- 1 1/2 cups chicken broth
- 1/2 tsp apple cider vinegar
- 1/4 tsp salt
- Dash of freshly ground red pepper
- 2 tbsp fresh basil, chopped

Directions

- Peel and crush garlic and set aside. Leaving crushed or minced garlic for at least 5-10 minutes after crushing helps maximize its health-protective effects.
- While health-promoting compounds are forming in crushed garlic, combine shallots, tomatoes, chicken broth, and apple cider vinegar in a blender or food processor and process until smooth.
- Heat olive oil in a large nonstick saucepan over medium heat. Add garlic and cook about 30 seconds, stirring constantly.
- Add tomato mixture, and bring to a boil. Turn off heat and stir in basil. Serve hot.

Broccoli and Barley Soup

Provided that you're not allergic or sensitive to gluten, this delicious and highly nutritious dish may help alleviate your asthma symptoms. The broccoli in this soup contains certain antioxidant compounds that help control the airway inflammation associated with bronchial asthma. The stewed tomatoes contain lycopene which has been shown to reduce lung inflammation. In addition, tomatoes are packed with the asthma-nutrients beta-carotene, vitamin C, and potassium. Also thyme and marjoram, which are used to add flavor to this soup, may be helpful for people with asthma as they contain ursolic acid which is thought to alleviate asthma by inhibiting histamine release from mast cells.

6 servings

Ingredients

- 1/4 cup yellow onion, chopped
- 1 small carrot, peeled and diced
- 1 rib organic celery, finely chopped
- 1 tbsp extra virgin olive oil
- 4 cups small, organic broccoli florets
- 1/2 cup pearled barley, cooked

- 5 cups vegetable broth
- 1 can (14 1/2 oz) stewed tomatoes
- 4 cloves garlic, minced
- 1/4 tsp dried marjoram
- 1 tsp thyme
- Salt and pepper, to taste

Directions

- In a stock pot, cook onion in olive oil over medium heat for 4-5 minutes until soft.
- Add vegetable broth and bring to a boil. Reduce to a simmer and add celery and carrots along with broccoli florets. Cover and let simmer until carrots and broccoli florets are tender.
- Add cooked barley, canned tomatoes, garlic, marjoram, and thyme. Let simmer another minute or two.
- Season with salt and pepper. Serve warm.